Words out of Silence

60 Days in Solitude

Bok

NON-DUALITY PRESS

Non-Duality Press is an Imprint of

newharbingerpublications, inc.
5674 Shattuck Avenue · Oakland CA 94609 · USA
800-748-6273 · fax 510-652-5472
www.newharbinger.com

ISBN: 978-1-908664-50-1
www.newharbinger.com

Without thought, you would always be here and now.
There would be no way to be anywhere else.
You must come to understand the nature of thought.
Why? Because thought happens.

Bok

Sixty days can feel like a long time.

Sixty days ALONE can feel like a really long time.

Sixty days ALONE in SILENCE can feel like... ETERNITY.

Dear A,

I leave for my 60-day retreat tomorrow. I'm nervous. I don't feel ready, but then I think, will I ever feel ready? I doubt it. Just have to jump in, I guess.

I am passionately interested in self-realization, as you know. My mind can't quite grasp the nature of it, but I've had a number of extraordinary experiences that have left an unforgettable taste in my mouth. Everything else in my life now turns back to this search. All is a means to this end. Every moment.

The idea of doing a long solo retreat has been growing in me for some time. Having done silent retreats with various spiritual teachers for about a decade now gives me some comfort, but 60 days alone in silence feels like a whole new level, and with that comes a whole new level of anxiety.

I plan on meditating when I first wake up, but other than that, I want to follow the whim of the moment. This is a little risky I think, not to have more structure, but I really want to notice, as I become more sensitive, where the body/mind/spirit moves me. I am bringing a book of Rumi for inspiration, and also the white orchid that you gave me, to remind me of your beauty.

Apparently, my little cabin is called "Most Secret" and is on the side of a hill overlooking a forest of pine trees and redwoods. It's one of a group of isolated cabins used specifically there for individual retreats. Down the hill from the cabin is a large creek that I can take my daily walks by, or climb back into the wild hills where deer and mountain lions co-exist.

My gracious hosts tell me the only time I'll be aware of them is when they ring the meal bell, alerting me that my food is ready by the washrooms. Other than that, it's just me in the mirror.

Wish me luck!

With Love, Bok

On the morning of April 23rd, I drove into the mountains just east of Santa Cruz, California and arrived at the Vajrapani Retreat Center late in the afternoon.

I parked my car and ascended a long set of wooden stairs to a tiny cabin at the top of the ridge. As the sun set, I reluctantly closed the cabin door to begin my sixty-day silent retreat.

Retreat

Day 1

I close the cabin door.

Not a word for 60 days.

I am alone.

Nausea. Overwhelming nausea.

I am gripped with fear.

I don't know if I can do this.

I'm sure I can't.

What was I thinking?

If I don't face this fear right now, I am done.

I sit.

I take out a pen and paper.

Why am I here?

Why AM I here?

To LOSE myself in the mystery of existence

Day 2

It's only the second day.
I want to go home.
There's nothing to do here.
No yoga classes.
No teachers to focus on.
No group meals.
There's nothing to do.
There's simply nothing to do.
Whenever I have this thought,
the unknown looms
and I feel the urge to puke.
Why am I here?

Why AM I here?

☾

To FIND myself in the mystery of existence

Day 3

When out of nowhere,
the breath makes itself evident,
and you desire nothing more than to listen to yourself
breathe,
something has fallen away,
for now.
This is a place of peace.

Trust the breath
It has no agenda
The breath is true
Through and through

☽

Breath is like my meditation belay.
It allows me to climb high with confidence
AND
It allows me to let go and fall without fear.

Day 4

I am here
I am still
I am at your mercy
Show me the way

I'm writing, I think.
I hear birds, I think.
The temperature is perfect, I think.
Only because I think.
Otherwise, who knows what's going on.

Day 5

Don't fool yourself thinking,
"I wish I had more time."
Even here in retreat,
where there's nothing to do,
I still think,
"I don't have enough time."
Amazingly, this thought still arises
and the anxiety right along with it.

I can't ever know what's best for another.
What's best for me is I don't know.
I think I know what's best for me
I think I know what's best
I think I know
I think
I

The "I" thought is powerful enough to create a "person".

Day 6

I'm on retreat.
I should take advantage of this time and do something.
Guess what?
I don't want to do anything.
Is there time for that?

☾

Just breathe, inquire, listen.

Day 7

The best thing about Silence—
It does all the work.
This is a good thing for a lazy loot like me.

If I had to pay for breath,
I'd spend every penny I had on it,
and I'd be a rich man.

Day 8

What is it about a path through the woods?

Day 9

What have I done to deserve this beauty?
Nothing.

Day 10

Bok, Bok.
Who's there?

Day 11

When feeling stuck
like a stick on the mud bank
of a rushing stream,
don't worry,
be patient,
and pray for rain.

There is no time to wallow in suffering.
There is too much joy, beauty, and love to be had.
And yet, here I sit in my perfect little cabin
with my perfect little orchid,
suffering.

Beauty takes precedence over suffering.

Day 12

What is "The Truth"?
Nothing more than what is happening right now
without interpretation.
Man making marks on paper.
"Man" sounds an awful lot like an interpretation to me.
"Paper"?
"Marks"?
Uh, oh.

Day 13

My teacher said, "Just feel into it."
Into what?
This sense of I am.
This sense of I am?
Yes.
Talk about vague. This was the definition of vague.
And yet, I said OK.
I knew, somehow, what he meant.
No, that's wrong,
I didn't know what he meant,
but whatever said OK knew.

☾

I am like a fly resting on a clear window pane,
looking out into the beautiful world,
wondering,
"What is stopping me?"

Perhaps it's like unfolding a sheet.
Without me, no unfolding. Without the sheet, no unfolding.
It takes both of us.
You can't say which is unfolding, me or the sheet.
So act as I wish and watch the great drama play out,
or don't act and watch the great drama play out.
Only thoughts say that it should be other than it is.

Day 14

Right now, all is well.
How could it be any other way?

Day 15

There is nothing I can accomplish in the world
that will give me a sense of lasting peace.
This I know.
Just look at your life. Just for a second.
It's always the next thing, isn't it?
No shame. No shame.

The trunk holds up the leaves so they may dance,
but the trunk never moves.

Dear A

As week 3 begins here, I feel like a chapter has come to an end, and a new one is beginning. My days have become simpler here, if that's possible. This feels like I'm in the meat of the retreat now. I'm doing a great deal of meditating, both lying on my back and sitting. This is not planned. I just go where the rhythm takes me. I seem to sit and eat and do written self-inquiry into the simple yet perplexing question of being, like "Who is afraid of dying? Who is meditating? What is attention? Who hears thought?" And on and on.

Nothing hangs on very long here. No state I mean. Any problematic state quickly becomes unbearable and forces me into inquiry. In this setting, it is quite clear, quite quickly when I'm lost in a troubling thought. What was only moments before a world of beauty and peace, now becomes a torture chamber, and all that's changed is my thinking. Last night I was in hell, today is lovely. Right now is lovely. Writing to you is lovely.

It has been raining almost non-stop since I've been here. At least a portion of everyday has seen showers. It's quite beautiful, and chilly up here. My little cabin is warm and cozy, and I feel very at home. Today was filled with such beauty. I spent much of it crying with a broken open heart.

From my little outdoor porch, I get to see all sorts of cool creatures. I have squirrels and blue jays, hummingbirds and butterflies, bobcats and coyotes, and everyday a family of deer come down and feed just below me. Mom and Dad and three little fellas. They don't seem afraid of me except when I move, then they freeze "like deer in headlights", and then hop away like they were on pogo sticks. Have you ever seen deer hop? It's truly bizarre. You'd think they'd run, but no. I love the squirrels and blue jays too. Blue jays find food, then go and hide it in different places till later. I know where their food is.

Oh, A, the orchid is dying. It was thriving until just a few days ago, and now it's dying. I don't know what to do. We had a little heatwave here and that may have done her in, I don't know. It also says on the instructions that it needs fertilizer which I don't have. It's been so beautiful, and still is, and it is a bit heartbreaking to see it wilting. But that's what is. I do what I can, with love, and let life take its course.

There's no way I could explain to you how subtly mysterious this trust in life has become here - moving the way it wants, doing what it wants, wondering why, then finding out. I can't really explain it. I know that this strange process - which is only strange because "I" can't understand it - is going along just fine and perfectly.

Try this, A. Just sit down for a second, take a few breaths to relax, and then ponder this sense of being alive. Don't think about it, but feel into it. What is this mysterious sense of existence, of being alive? That, my dear, is a large doorway. Ponder it, feel it, question it, play with it, wonder about it, this sense of being, this subtle mysterious sense of being alive. It's closer than anything you can look for. You must get very quiet inside and slowly feel your way into it. But be careful, you may fall in love with it. After all, it might be you.

I love you to bits - B

Day 16

Is there anything more beautiful
than the effortlessness of a tributary joining a stream?
Maybe only the passion
with which water falls over an edge.

I find that I have been living the fear of attachment
as opposed to living the understanding of non-attachment.
A subtle but huge difference.

Day 17

I heard the phone ringing in my cabin.
I rushed home to get it.
It was a bird in the tree calling me home.
Then I remembered, I don't have a phone.

I thought I had to have more energy, better health,
more meditation, etc.
All just thoughts, when no, it's been perfect, every moment,
to lead to where I Am.
It's just a shut up and wake up kind of thing.

It's more confusion than ignorance or fear.

Day 18

Mint tea and inquiry?
Certainly.

I don't know what to do

Who doesn't?

I don't

Who am I?

I don't know

Who doesn't know?

I don't

Who am I?

A thought

A thought that says, "I don't"

Who am I without that thought?

I don't know

Without that thought?

Presence

Without that thought?

Being

Without that thought?

I

Without that thought?

Pure perception

Without that thought?

Everything

Without that thought?

Nothing

Without that thought?

☾

Day 19

Birds sing for our enlightenment.
Different pitches and rhythms all designed to wake us up.
They just keep singing,
hoping one day we'll hear them just so.

This sense of being.
What is it?
What is all this taking place within?
What is aware of sounds and sight and movement and
breath and thought all at once?
Just sitting here, aware.

Day 20

With the vision turned in,
I feel like a child embarrassed to look out.
I turn my shy gaze onto the world,
careful not to disturb the beauty
but anxious to get a quick peek.

Day 21

The personality wants recognition.
The space that I am doesn't care.

Day 22

When I have the thought
"I have to hold onto this sense of peace",
I get desperate,
scared it might go,
insecure,
wild-eyed,
clutching,
I force it,
I fake it,
and I conjure it falsely.
I imagine it's my doing.

What is surrender?

Surrender is letting go, it is giving up, it is letting down my
guard and trusting life. Surrender is trust in The Mystery,
surrender is believing all my teachers and trusting what
they have told me is true, surrender is dropping everything,
all stories, all defenses, all excuses and saying now. Why
not, now? Surrender is choosing love over fear, surrender
is letting life live me, surrender is true peace and love.
Surrender is the end of arrogance, the end of believing that
I'm the one wise enough to run this life. Surrender is the end
of me. Surrender means saying enough is enough. I don't
know what to do, here, it's your turn. With love, turning over
my life to something larger. Surrender is the end of fear and
holding. Surrender is trust. Surrender is knowing that "what
is" is always the right thing. Surrender is trusting the pain
and the joy. Surrender is relief. A huge relief. I can't do it.
Can you? Please.

☾

Day 23

Nothing to do.
Nothing to be.
No one to become.
What more could you ask for?
Make a list, then read aloud the misery of your life.
Scratch off one by one and feel the freedom flow
through your body a little each time.
And wonder,
What do I really want?
What tightens my belly and what makes it shake with
laughter?
What causes me to spit poison at my loved ones
and what frees up my heart to hold them in their misery?
What do I want to say to myself on my death bed?
What might be the last words I say to myself
as the window of consciousness closes one final time?
Maybe there's nothing to say. Maybe there's just a smile.
Wouldn't that be a fortunate life?
Indeed!

Stick to the breath and dissolve.

Day 24

The moment of realization comes.
A mosquito buzzes in my ear.
I take a swipe at it.
Shit! I missed it.

Body holds tension between reality and dream.

Day 25

The body is tight, sore, and miserable.
It's acting as if there's a coup about.

It feels like a habit of packaging.
Thoughts sound like they're in the head
so the "listener" assumes they're part of the body
and then hears "I",
so assumes the body/mind must be the "I".

Day 26

When I am at peace,
there is nothing more beautiful than solitude
in my little cabin.
When I am not at peace,
there is nothing more hellish than solitude in my little cabin.
The cabin hasn't changed.

☾

I am starving to drown in the sweetness of the Divine.

I can hear it calling all around.

A bird's song, a western wind,

a leaf-rustling, tree-swaying sound.

I want to be inside, on the inside, seeing from the inside,

to be a part of the mystical world of lovers

that poetry and satsang sing of.

The taste is on the back of my tongue somewhere,

but I can't get at it with my tongue.

I can only scratch and claw with bloody breath,

desperate to be quiet enough to be invited into the big hall

where God is throwing a silent festival

that can be heard throughout the galaxies.

I'll do anything.

I'll serve the wine, I'll cook the food, I'll hang up coats.

Just let me peek into the great hall.

And maybe, if I'm lucky, they'll mistake me for a guest

and invite me in.

Once in, who's going to say anything?

Day 27

Now what?

I don't know what to do. I don't want to do anything.

I want to give up. I want to be taken.

I

I

I

Does anyone hear me?

Do I hear me?

Does it hear me?

Am I I?

Who am I?

What am I?

Does anything need doing?

Have I not done enough undoing?

I guess not.

I'm still making movies.

The sprockets are still spinning.

I can only hope the dimmer switch

has been cranked some to the left

and now the fan turns slower.

What can I do to turn that switch until I hear it click?

Maybe nothing.

Maybe the power needs to be cut to the house altogether.

At the Source.

Call the power company.

I want off the grid.

Day 28

My interest in thought seems to always be there,
lurking,
waiting,
like a mouse in a kitchen.
It doesn't seem to matter how well I clean up,
whenever I turn my back,
it steals in
and finds the smallest crumbs,
then leaves its droppings.

Frustrated, powerless, confused, tired.
I wonder what I've done wrong.
I wonder why I can't stop paying attention to thought.

Day 29

It's like the mind expects something more to happen
so it starts searching and suggesting,
and we get lured back in by it.
It wants fireworks
and this is quiet.

☾

Seeing through the eyes of a child
Seeing through the I's of a grown up

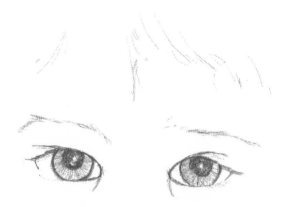

Day 30

I am the immovable backdrop of all that happens.
I am that feeling that's always been there,
that sense of me.

Dear A,

Things haven't been so easy for me lately. Last week I hit a real rough patch. Lots of doubt, fear and suffering. A lovely recipe, you can imagine. And no way to get away from it here. I have to simply squirm and wait for a clearing. But remarkably, it's like a passing storm. Violent and blustery, and then simply gone, and the clear sky that appears afterward seems brighter than ever. It's always remarkable to me how this happens. How it can seem so bleak and so real, and then pop, I'm out in the clear, looking up at the night sky with all its shining stars, grateful just to be.

I have spent most of my time these last few days staring at nothing in particular, immersed in the sense of I Am, this mysterious sense of being, of being alive. This happened quite suddenly a few days ago and has not let go of me since. It seems every time I look at something, I end up just staring at it for god knows how long. During that time, my attention pulls into the solar plexus, and I just experience my breathing as I gently inquire deeper into this sense of being. It's beautiful.

As the silence deepens for me here, I find myself many days just sitting for hours at a time, simply listening to the world outside and inside. It's that feeling of listening with your entire being. I feel my breath and hear it, I hear birds, I hear the river, the wind, the silence itself, and feel that mysterious sense of existence. Truly simple and beautiful. Only a thought that I attach to pulls me out of the wonder. Nothing else.

One thing I really want to encourage you to try is to do a sincere questioning of what this sense of "I" is. Meaning: My thoughts? My feelings? My body? It's actually pretty obvious when looked at closely that this thing I call "I" can't be any of those things I just mentioned, so what's left? The only thing that is always present and always has been, is this sense of being. Now, it's still a bit of a mind bender for me to really know that's who I am, but there isn't anything else. I think it's important to have a deep intellectual conviction that this is true. It then really opens up the mind and senses to a different possibility. Plus, it partially breaks the bondage over changing states of mind and physicality.

I've been reading lots of Rumi. Wow! Love the guy. I love him like I love you. I don't know either of you really, but your essence brings me joy. What a madman.

I've been writing lots of poetry myself. I feel like writing poetry is such a natural fit for my being. My creativity has always come like quick-fire, hot and instant (like oatmeal), and poetry can just flash out of me using words and images and insights. I don't like to hold onto the creative process generally for the long haul, like writing novels or films, or other long projects. I am too fickle in nature for long processes. (Irony noted that I'm alone in a cabin for two months doing a looonnnngggggg process).

I've been amazed that my gusto for meditating and questioning this existence has only increased since being here. It's really all I do everyday basically, and I'm amazed I haven't burned out yet. But there seems to be no end to this fire, at least not until I know who I am without doubt. Maybe then the fire will turn into a cozy ember in the heart that will warm me until I die. I don't know.

There comes a point in meditation, A, where you are so relaxed and there's nothing more to do, so you just rest in the sense of being, hearing your breath, the birds outside, everything, listening to life with your entire being, and there you sit, totally at ease and at peace, waiting to be taken. So the term 'waiting without waiting', as Jean Klein puts it. It describes it perfectly, because the state of rest is so profound, there is no anxiousness of waiting, yet there's this slight knowing that you are waiting.

We are approaching summer and the days are getting longer. Some days seem interminable or is it just me? My orchid is still here. I don't know if it's living or just here, dead, waiting? It doesn't look good, but I sense life in it. I don't want to pull the plug too quickly. What's the rush anyway? It's good to have something to care for.

Loving you, Bob

Day 31

What would birds do without trees?

What's the story with animals?
All they seem to do is look for food.
Are they really that hungry?
Is there just nothing else to do?
Are they eating so they don't have to face their problems?
And what are their problems?
The only one I can see is, they don't seem to have
enough food.
Can somebody help me here?

Day 32

If I love, all else is irrelevant.

☽

Love or thought, pick one.

Day 33

The mind is like a haunted house at an amusement park.
The first time through,
you can hardly take your hands from your face,
the fear so constant and overwhelming.
But after many times through,
with your eyes gradually more open,
you reach a point where you can hardly contain the laughter
as the sheets jump from the corners,
pretending to be ghosts.

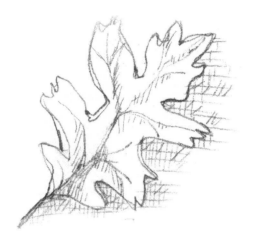

The mind wants the mind to be quieter.
One of its sneaky tricks.

Day 34

I've never done anything for so long in my life
with such focus and passion and intensity,
and had such few results.

I think.

☾

Self-realization is apparently kinda funny in that
just because you go after it,
doesn't mean you're going to get it.
It's sort of like being a single woman at a wedding
when it comes time for the bouquet toss.
Your job is to get yourself in the best position possible.
Where the bouquet actually goes is anyone's guess.
But if you're not in good position, you can forget it.
Usually.

Day 35

Do bugs know where they're going?

Sometimes I like to walk alongside a flying ladybug
and put out my hand
and pretend I'm an aircraft carrier.

Day 36

I expect no one to understand my life.
I really don't understand my life, I just live it.
To understand it implies that it makes sense to me,
which it does in a way,
but more I just follow the flow of passion and love,
and trust where I'm going.
In that sense, I'm as clueless as everyone else
how I ended up here,
and yet being here feels totally and utterly right.

We try to understand life as a Whole
but it doesn't exist as a Whole,
only moment to moment.

Day 37

Speak not at all
unless it is your heart insisting.
Love, laugh and play.
Be silent.

Who is writing now
as the pen is sliding across the page
is there a sense of someone doing this
or is it just happening
all the thoughts are about
what's going down on the page here
so there is no "I" thought
but there is something that is witnessing this process
which doesn't really feel involved.
Now, I say, "I just wrote that."

Day 38

Here moment to moment,
feeling the flow of life and moving as it,
trusting, not knowing, no names, no ideas, just life,
nothing as a stage to something else,
just here now and constantly surprised.

I realized today
that of all the things I could be doing
and all the places I could be,
this is where I want to be more than anywhere else.

Imagine that!

Everything reminds me that I Am.
Everything is because I Am.

Day 39

Intellectual understanding that you are not the body
will not cure the suffering man of body identification.
Certainly not.
Just as a sip of water will not quench a thirsty man.
But take many sips from the same cup
and soon you may find the desire for more gone.
Then, what is there left to do
but relax in the sun and wait to be burned.

☾

Without the mind telling me so,
where am I?

Without thought,
I don't know what I am.
I appear to still be,
but as what,
I don't know.

Without thought,
there is no evidence that I am anyone,
only that I AM.

Day 40

I cried for the happiness that was my life.
I cried for the sorrow that became my life.
And I cry for the gratitude that is my life now.

Day 41

To love what is
is the only sane choice.

Find your own language for this.
Find your own words.
Find words that stir you.

Day 42

They tell me that I am the wetness of a grand
mountain reservoir,
yet I can't speak I'm so parched with thirst.
They tell me I'm the apple in the pig's mouth
at the center of a great banquet feast,
yet I feel the ravenous hunger of a starving tiger.
They tell me that I'm the North Star in a Universe
of galaxies,
yet I see only darkness on all sides.
They tell me I'm just dreaming and to wake up,
yet I can't hear them over my snoring.
They tell me the love of the mystical union is indescribable,
yet I clutch at them to give me the secret.
They tell me to just stop and see.
That's it, just stop and you'll see.
And I do.
I stop, and I see, only me, looking, looking, looking…

☾

The mind is not for seeing truth,
but for recognizing that which isn't true and dispelling it.
Like a bouncer.

Day 43

If your path feels like a crooked one,
gently pull on both ends for a second,
just to see the true nature of it.
And then let go.

Day 44

Is any thought true?
Who knows, it's gone.

What?

Dear A,

Hi, it's another morning. I was just thinking, isn't it wild that we're so hot inside. We're almost 100 degrees in there. You know how hot it feels when it's 100 degrees out, not to mention humid, I mean, we're how much percent water? Talk about humid! We are one steamy creature.

I am torn, A, between two desires: one - to be a self-realized human being and two - to be a world-renowned squirrel expert. They are the most amazing creatures. The way they leap from branch to branch, tree to tree, ground to tree, is amazing. They always find purchase (I've been dying to use that word). And their tails are simply sublime. They sort of fade away to nothing, so much so that you can see through the last portion of it, but it's still there. It doesn't appear possible. And I wish I knew how they held so tightly and assuredly to whatever they desire. Their claws must be something else. Well, I guess based on my current enthusiasm, I'll have to choose #2 from the above list - Squirrel Master.

Many many weeks in, and I feel this deep reservoir of silence and peace at the center of my being that is sweet beyond words. I can't believe how much faith I have in just sticking to the sense of I Am. I know to my soul - whatever that is - that that's enough. And I love that faith and trust.

Generally, I find the hardest mind-states for me not to be the single-story narratives, but more when my mind is jumping from thing to thing to thing, staying on each subject for a few thoughts, then moving on. Drives me frickin' crazy. Of course, this isn't quite accurate, for this is what the mind does habitually. It's not the mind jumping around that drives me crazy, but my interest in it that is so exhausting.

The mind seems to shuffle fairly randomly through a Rolodex of old thoughts, testing, testing, until we bite. Then the story begins, with that thought. Until we bite, it just keeps scanning the files. This is why it is so important to know 'your' mind. If you know it inside and out, there is nothing it can find that will make you bite. It's like knowing all the secrets of a great magician. Just can't fool you anymore. And at some point, it seems to pretty much give up. Or at least slow down.

Another thing, when I really look closely, it is obvious beyond any doubt that I have absolutely no control over this moment Now. How could I? It is gone and gone and gone OR now and now and now. How could I have any control and moreover, who is there to have any control now and now and now? If this moment is all there ever is, when is there time for me? And then we extrapolate - to all nows, now, only now, ongoing nows in the now. The illusion of control of anything is just that. Illusion. Scary? Maybe at first but such a relief when the futility is truly seen. Then fear turns to freedom.

Don't take my word for it - ever!
Lovely You, Bok

Day 45

I used to think it was a compliment
to be called complicated
and an insult to be called simple.

IT is complex.
I AM simple.

Day 46

What does it matter
where I am or what I'm doing,
as long as I'm present?
I mean, really?

Let the body be
Let the mind be
Rest in being

Day 47

I'm not depressed.
I'm not sad.
I don't know what I am.
This is new.
I want to call it something, but nothing comes.
The old names seem inappropriate.
It's almost like confusion but it's not.
It's almost like boredom but it's not.
It's almost like depression but it's not.
This underlying silence makes all those too dramatic.
This is simpler.
Deeper.
Older.
It just doesn't know.

Who doesn't long to hear,
from a power greater than themselves,
"You're going to be OK."

Day 48

The moth had been in here for days.

On the wall. At the window. On the ceiling.

Night. Day.

How had this become his world?

He thinks he remembers being free.

Now this.

Sometimes he would flutter for hours in front of the window

looking out at his dream world.

It must be only a dream, he thought, or else why can't I

have it?

There it is. With nothing in between.

And yet, I remain enclosed. In prison. In dreaming.

And then, with no warning,

I grabbed him, opened the door and released him.

And again, he was free.

Out of nowhere. For no reason. Only longing.

And it was his.

The only price: his prison.

I may just sit here at this table
staring out the window for the next week.
What else is there to do?
Is there anything to accomplish?
How will I know if I've accomplished something?
Leaving here broken?
I don't want to be together.
I want to walk in the world without a clue,
and let life come to me.

Day 49

Have you ever seen a tree with an imperfection?

Day 50

My instinct is always, just stop and let be.
No complications, no tricks, no strategies,
just stop and let be,
and drop in the question when it occurs—
Who am I?
This is what I always come back to.
The formula –
Breathe, Inquire, Listen.

☾

Day 51

I feel like an old rug
hung up and battered to get the dust out.
Apparently, there's still more dust.
I can only take the battering.
There's no fighting back.
Especially if I want to be used in the house.
So much dust. Gritty in the teeth.
I've spent seven weeks alone here in silence.
I will spend eight.
Then it's the world's turn to have its whacks at me.

Day 52

To die in the longing can be sweet, they say.
What choice have I got?
This is not a gift guaranteed like a gold watch on retirement.
This is not the longing of the horny teenager
who thinks it a lifetime between orgasms.
No, this is a longing that may see no quenching,
so if I'm not to die in the longing,
there is only desert.
Dry, hot, barren cynicism.
No place for the heart.
I can't do anymore for now.
I'm spent and flat on the ground,
waiting to be walked on by God.

I am a whirling of contradictions at the moment.

I feel tired,

then full of energy.

I'm clear as a bell,

then foggy as a San Francisco night.

I have great faith,

then greater doubt.

Full of understanding,

empty with despair.

Something is amiss.

Or nothing is amiss.

I don't know.

Day 53

What does it mean to give up the assumption
that there is any other time but Now?
What are the ramifications of truly understanding this?

Day 54

Free to know nothing.
Free not to impress.
Free not to compete.
Free to relax and love others for who they are
and be spontaneous in my interactions.
Free to thrive in not knowing.

Day 55

I long to be the clean mirror
to reflect the mystery without blemish.
To see clearly,
as light pouring through me unclouded, unchecked.
As beauty and unity,
leaving only a gasp of awe and utter amazement.
On the face of the mirror, the reflection the same
Awe!
Awe!
Don't look, look, don't look.
How can I not?
How can I avert my eyes?

☾

Superiority is in the mind.
Simplicity is in the heart.

Day 56

There is no room for Me in Presence.

Day 57

God, what a relief to know nothing
and consequently, be nobody.

Day 58

It seems that everything is just an idea
except raw perception
and this sense of being.

Life
Never-ending Life.
I Am coming to Life everywhere I look.

Make no mistake,
Everything is profound.

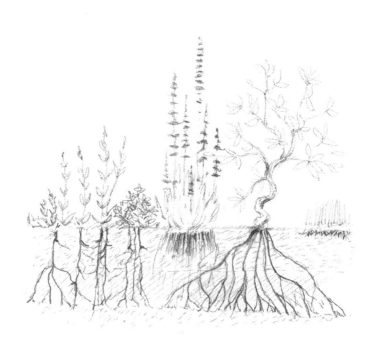

Day 59

In the present, I'm never anything I think.

Nothing more comes.
I am empty now like a wine barrel that's been tapped out.
Nothing remains inside
and that nothing is quiet and at rest.
Now I wait to be filled again,
hoping that the wine-maker
has a particularly rare vintage in mind.

Day 60

The mind is a butterfly.
I am the sky.

Dear A,

Miracle of all miracles - the orchid has come back
to life and is in full bloom. I'm coming home.

Bok

☾

Notice attachment and let it go.
Back to the breath, or awareness, or just go wide into being.
Not much effort, just widen out and move slightly away.
Let it go gently with no story.

Every moment is fresh and untouched.

It doesn't matter what came before
or how attached you just were to a story.
The second you're out, you're free.
Unblemished.
As though nothing had happened, because it didn't.

At your core, there is a profound silence.
A silence that is playful, free and at peace.
If you can't feel it, find it.
Look with gentleness, curiosity, and persistence.
Use your breath.
Don't wait.

So in the end, dear friends,
Bok did not LOSE himself or FIND himself
in the mystery of existence as he had hoped,
but instead,
found himself AS the mystery of existence.
Who could have guessed?

THE NOW

The Story of Bok

The name Bok was given to me by my god-daughter,
Surya, as soon as she was old enough to speak, around 2.
Actually, my full name was The Bok, as if I was some Dr.
Seuss character or an alien race from a Star Trek episode.
When I would visit her home, she would call out, "The
Bok is here!" When she was old enough to understand
my question, probably around 4, I asked her why she
called me The Bok, and she said, very logically, "Because
that's your name." How could I argue with that?

When I closed the door on my little cabin for 60
days of silence, it seemed quite natural that my pen
name for the retreat would be Bok. My Zen teacher
of many years used to talk of his favorite Zen monk,
Bankei, from way back when. My god-daughter would
say, "Oh Bokkie" when she thought I was being particularly silly. So it all fit, just right, for my time here.

The love of my god-daughter and the love of my
teacher were perfectly encapsulated in this simple name,
a name that warmed my heart and lit up my face
whenever I heard it, imagined it, or wrote it. It is good to
have a loving companion on such a lonely journey.

Thank You's (in chronological order)

William Crowell

Weaver Stevens

Marcie Jenner

Ramana Maharshi

Marvin Treiger

Catherine Ingram

Nisargadatta Maharaj

Jean Klein

Adyashanti

Byron Katie

And

Ava, Libby, & Helena, my silence muses

To my friend and editor, Arthur Jeon

Alexandra Burda, for her stunning sketches

To Catherine and Julian Noyce for believing in this book

And

To my wife, Fritzi, who is my playmate and partner

AND FINALLY to my dear boy, Conrad James,

who embodies two words for me: Committed Wonder.

For more information, you can contact me directly at:

TheBok23@gmail.com

or go to my website:

www.thebok.net

☾

Sketches by Alexandra Burda
www.AlexandraBurda.com